Forward

The motivating factor behind composing these etudes for finger style ukulele, is to address the ukulele player's desire to expand their right hand picking abilities. That's first and foremost, but in doing so, it helps to have left hand challenges and engaging music too. I have had a great time working toward this goal and these books are the result of a few years of intense composing, editing, playing and teaching these studies.

The easier, shorter ones are designed to get you warmed up and ready tickle the longer, more involved ones. Take them at your own pace and ease into any that give you problems. It helps sometimes to break a hard section down into individual measures that you loop over and over until ready to put back into the piece as a whole.

There is a lot of room for interpretation and I encourage each individual to find their own way through these. Play them as written, but then expand on them or finger them differently, transpose them, change the rhythmic feel, etc. The possibilities are endless!

I wish to thank my wife, Kristina for generously allowing me the space to work on this project and my many students who have given these puppies a whirl and tested them for me. My supportive family have always encouraged me to dive into this lifetime of music. This series of books is dedicated to my dear departed dad, Henry Weinberger, who loved music and in turn, instilled that love in me.

Cover Art ©2016 Joan Proudman
Contents ©2016 Jeffrey Weinberger

Ukulele Fingerstyle Etude #1
Jeffrey Weinberger

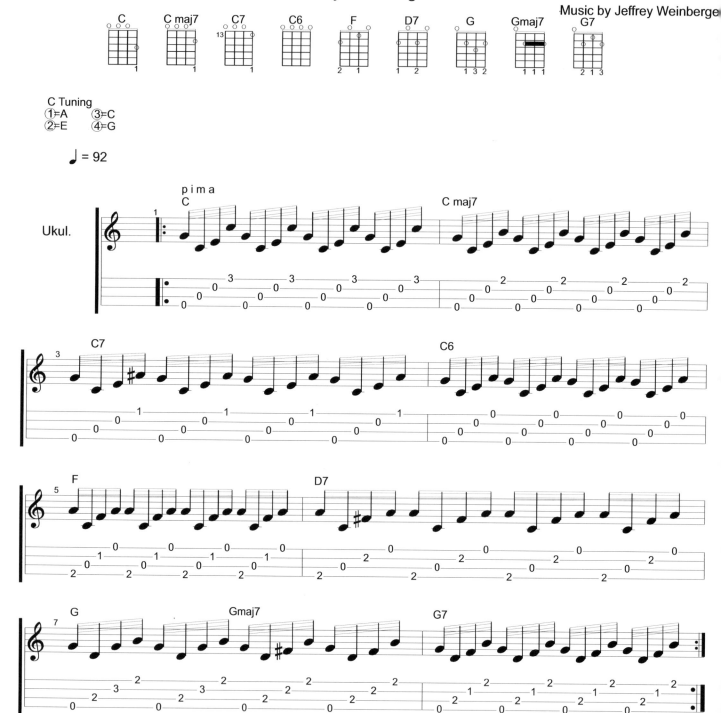

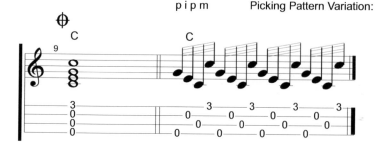

Uke Fingerstyle Etude #2

Music by Jeff Weinberger

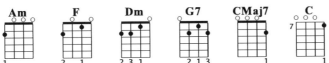

C Tuning
①= A ③= C
②= E ④= G

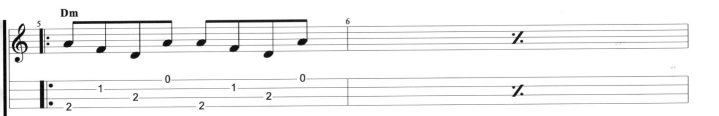

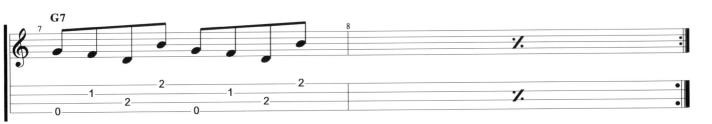

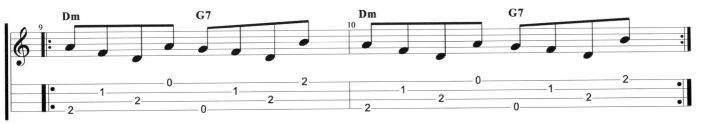

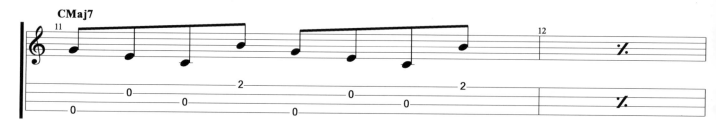

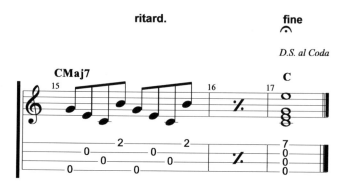

Uke Fingerstyle Etude #9 in C

Music by Jeff Weinberger

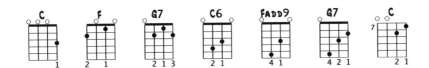

C Tuning
①= A ③= C
②= E ④= G

 = 123

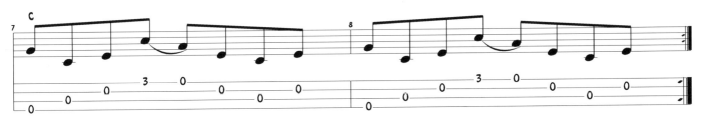

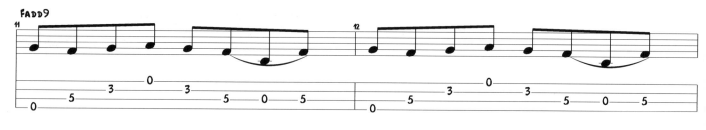

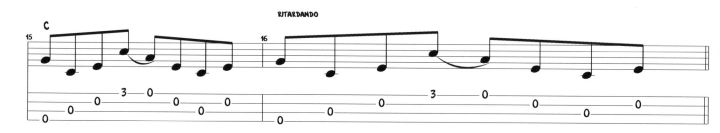
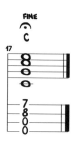

Etude 8/24/15 for Fingerstyle Ukulele

Music by Jeffrey Weinberger

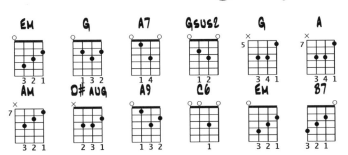

$\quad = 120$

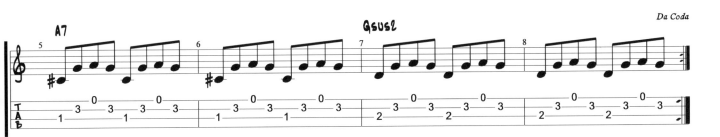

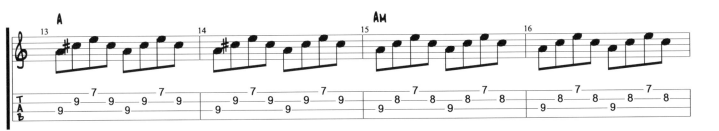

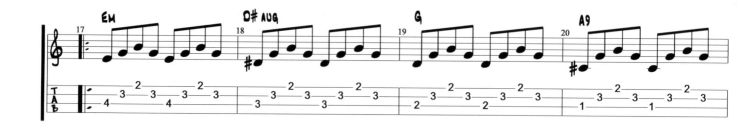

D.C. al Coda

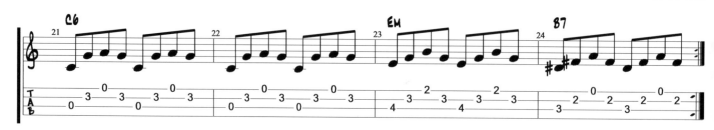

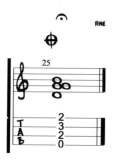

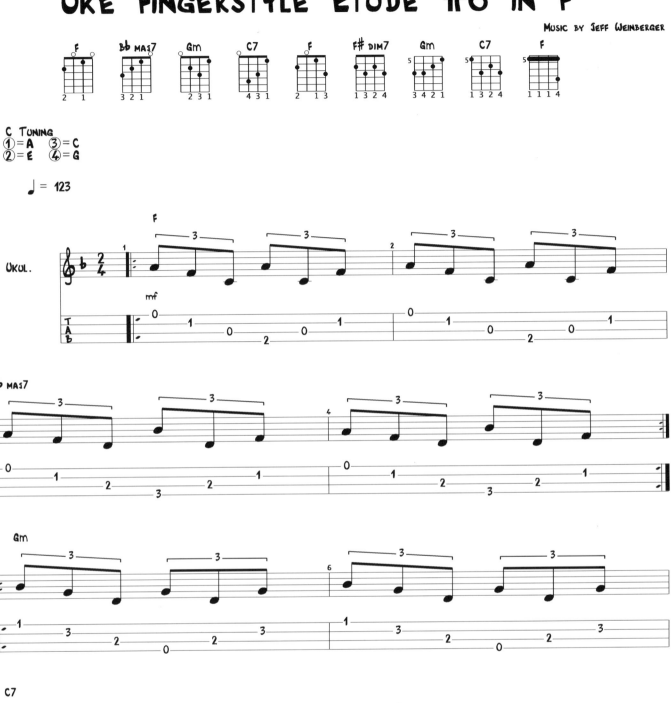

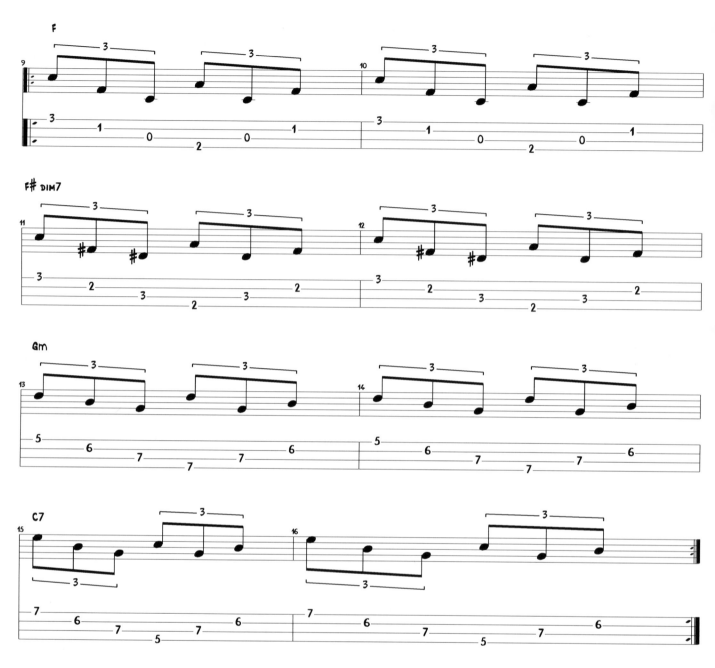
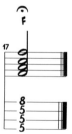

Uke Fingerstyle Etude 2/13/15

Music by Jeff Weinberger

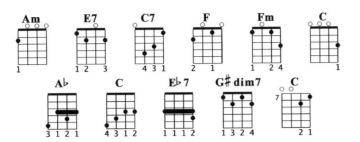

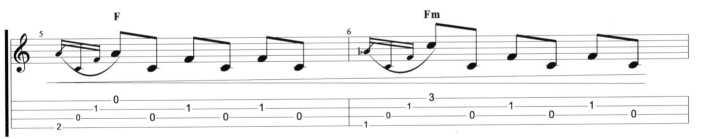

Uke Fingerstyle Etude #2

Music by Jeff Weinberger

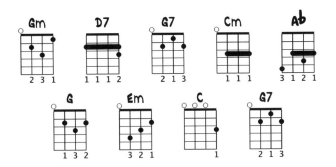

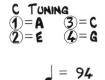

C Tuning
①= A ③= C
②= E ④= G

♩ = 94

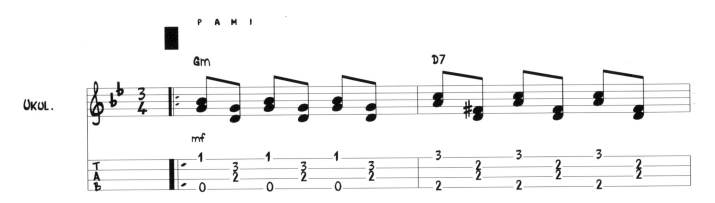

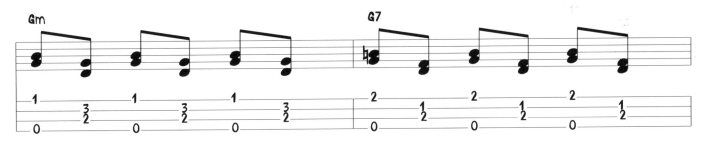

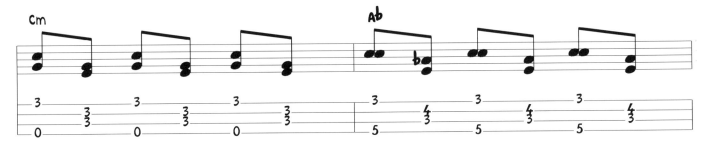

Uke Fingerstyle Etude #2

Music by Jeff Weinberger

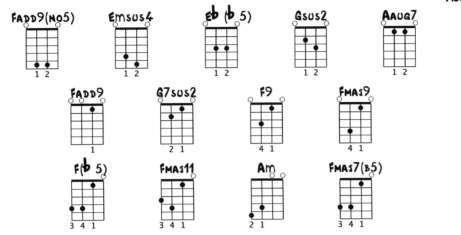

C Tuning
① = A   ③ = C
② = E   ④ = G

♩ = 143

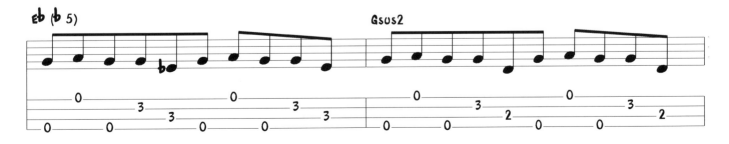

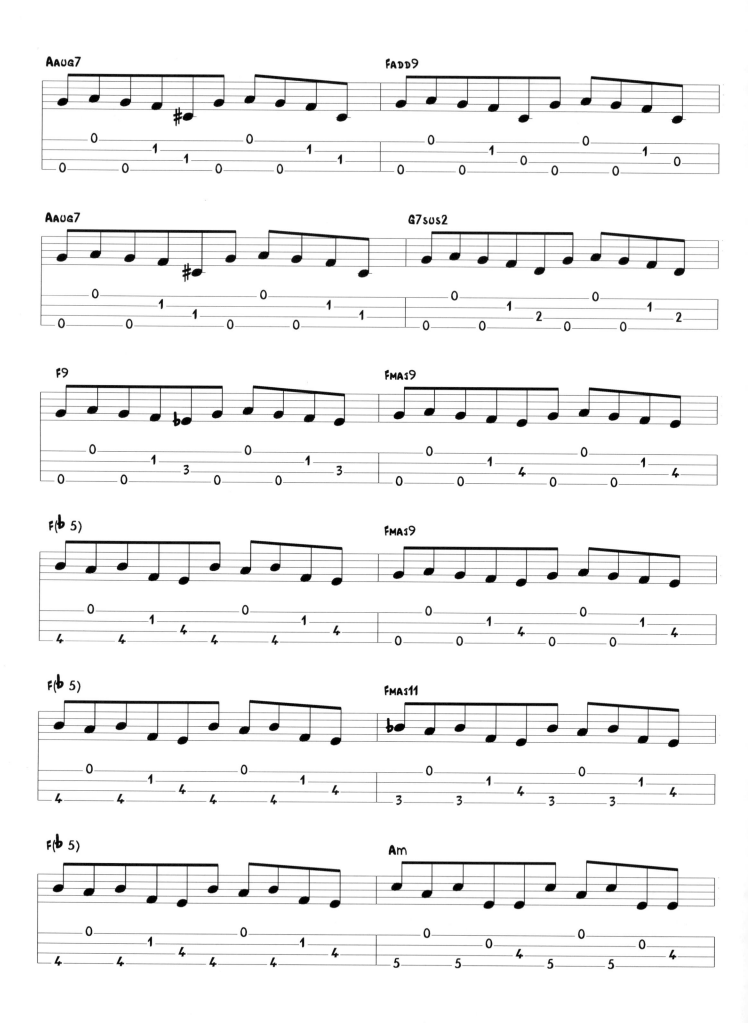

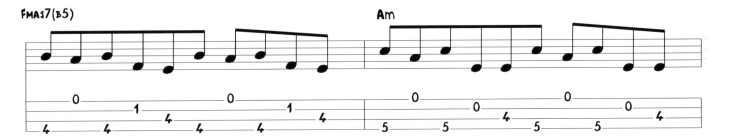

Etude in D for Fingerstyle Ukulele
GCEA Tuning

Music by Jeffrey Weinberger

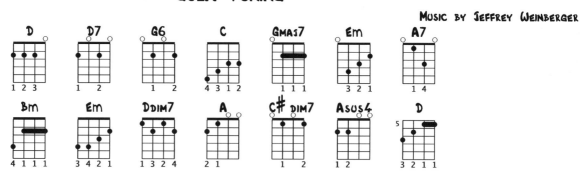

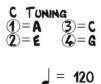

♩ = 120

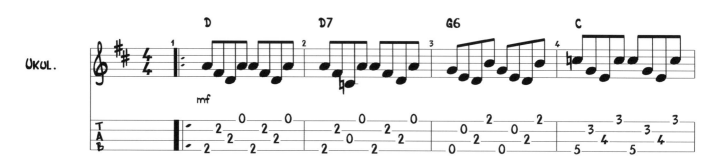

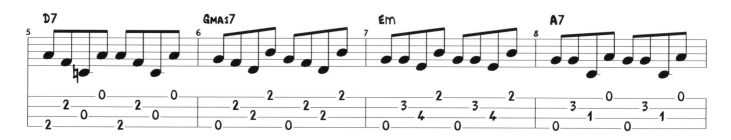

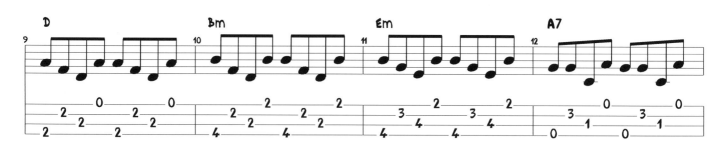

Etude in Dm

Music by Jeffrey Weinberger

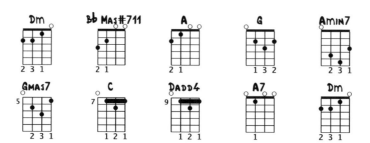

C Tuning
①= A ③= C
②= E ④= G

♩ = 74

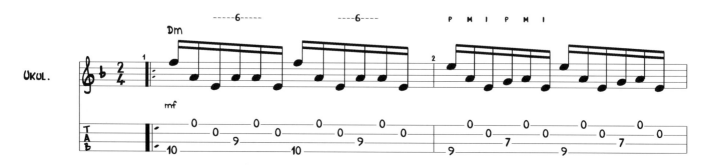

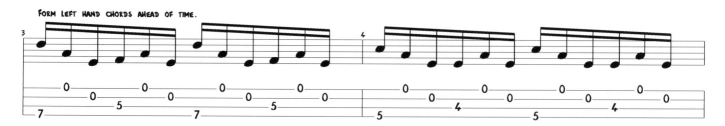

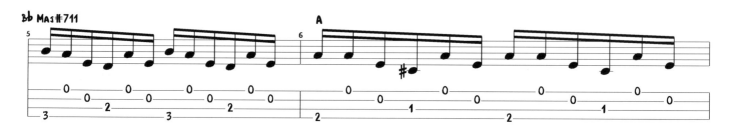

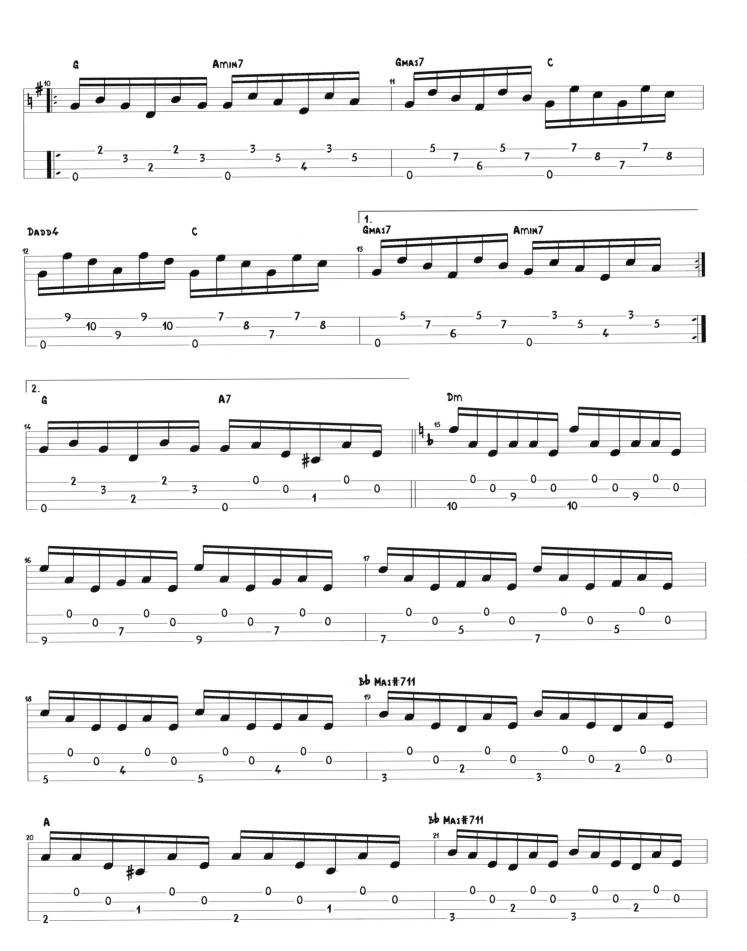

Performance Notes

Etude 1 in C is the first one I wrote for this collection several years ago. It makes a nice introduction for those new to fingerstyle uke playing and a nice warm up for those already familiar with the technique. The aim is to master the simple p i m a right hand pattern that I call the "straight down" pattern.

#2 in A minor is an early one also. For the Am to F chord change and back to Am, don't lift the left hand 2nd finger.

For the F to Dm chord change, don't lift the 1st or 2nd finger.

for the Dm to G7 chord change, don't lift the 1st finger.

This étude is designed to teach you the guitar fingerstyle pattern known as "Travis Picking" as popularized by Merle Travis, Chet Atkins, Tommy Emmanuel and many other legendary guitar pickers. The thumb travels between the G and C strings, creating a hypnotic, alternating pattern while the 1st finger consistently plays the E string and the 2nd finger takes care of the A string.

Another skill this etude was designed to develop is that of smooth chord changes. Make sure to leave the appropriate left hand fingers down to facilitate this. You are trying to achieve a singing, legato sound that rings and hasn't got too many breaks in between notes and chords. They should flow evenly from one to another. When I play in this style. I often think of Chopin and his singing piano sound.

This finger independence is a somewhat difficult skill at first, but well worth the effort. It is essential in learning classical music and also some popular music styles such as folk, country, bluegrass, etc.

#9 in C is mostly easy, but introduces a few "up the neck" chords and the pull off technique. For those unfamiliar with this, pluck the first note as usual, with the right hand, but then pull the left hand finger off the string to re-pluck it without touching it again with your right hand. This gives a smooth, flowing sound known as "legato".

Starting in m.9, the 3 note legatos are performed by doing a pull off as usual, but then slamming the left hand finger back down to the original fret from which it was pulled off from. This is known as a "hammer on" and is another of the legato techniques. You should get 3 notes with one pluck.

This will take practice and persistence for the beginner, but once mastered, raises the level of proficiency and expressiveness quite a bit. If you can do it well, you are not a beginner anymore!

Etude 8/24/15 in G is more recent and incorporates up the neck chords and more harmonically complex sounds. It shows the way to music beyond the simple major, minor and seventh chord. It does;t have a right hand picking pattern notated, but I would use p i m i

#6 in F uses yet more up the neck chord inversions and introduces counting in 2. It also has triplets. I like to pick it a m i p i m. The rhythm is "1 and ah 2 and ah" or "1 triplet 2 triplet" or "strawberry, strawberry". Whatever works for you!

Etude 2/13/15 is a favorite among my students who test drove it. It teaches the "roll" technique that is common in classical guitar music. The three grace notes are played in quick succession before the beat even starts. They lead into the 1st beat, which is an open A string. The final C chord is one of my favorite voicings of it.

This one has more detailed dynamics and the crescendo and decrescendo markings should be strictly observed. If unsure, just omit them for now and go back later and add them to give your performance a more emotive quality.

#2 in G minor uses a "pinch" technique where you play a thumb note and a finger note simultaneously. "ritardando" means to gradually slow down and the "bird's eye" symbol above the final chord is a fermata. That means to hold for an indefinite amount of time until the player or conductor decide it is time to silence it.

#2B in F has some pretty unusual chords. It also has a 5/4 time signature. You can subdivide this into 3 + 2 or 2 + 3 depending on your desired feel. 123 12 or 12 123. This is a fairly difficult one, but played fast, can dazzle the listener.

Etude in D has a lot of chords and 2 options for picking patterns. Try p i p i for a Chet Atkins/ Travis Picking feel or p m i a for a more challenging classical style. Getting to the final D chord cleanly may take some work.

The 10th and final Etude in D minor, will take a lot of concentration and focus to play flawlessly. The sextuplet rhythm is 6 fast, even notes over a single tap of the foot. I intended it to have some Gypsy Flamenco fire to it. Enjoy!

Jeff Weinberger is a Midcoast Maine based musician and educator who can be contacted through his website, www.jeffreyweinberger.com or via email at jeffrey.weinberger@maine.edu

You can also visit his Facebook page, Belfast Guitar and Ukulele Workshop. He is available for workshops, clinics and FaceTime lessons.

Besides music, he enjoys his family, gardening, cooking and long walks on the beach.

These études can be purchased together or separately as a hard copy or eBook at the above website. All contents copyright 2016.

Made in the USA
San Bernardino, CA
20 February 2016